D0870941

Pet Care

Cocker Spaniels

Kelley MacAulay & Bobbie Kalman

Photographs by Marc Crabtree

🌿 Crabtree Publishing Company

www.crabtreebooks.com

Cocker Spaniels

A Bobbie Kalman Book

Dedicated by Samantha Crabtree
To Kaleigh Ray Pope, the most precious little girl I know.

Editor-in-Chief
Bobbie Kalman

Writing team
Kelley MacAulay
Bobbie Kalman

Substantive editor
Kathryn Smithyman

Editors
Molly Aloian
Michael Hodge
Robin Johnson
Rebecca Sjonger

Design
Katherine Kantor

Production coordinator
Heather Fitzpatrick

Photo research
Crystal Foxton

Consultant
Dr. Michael A. Dutton, DVM, DABVP, Weare Animal Hospital,
www.weareanimalhospital.com

Special thanks to
Katherine Kantor, Alexander Makubuya, Lakme Mehta-Jones,
Owen Mehta-Jones, Shilpa Mehta-Jones, Samara Parent, Bailee Setikas,
Shelbi Setikas, Sheri Setikas, Katrina Sikkens, Michael Hill and Lacy-Lou,
Susan Fast and Casey, Lexi, Jack, Matty, and the puppies

Photographs
All photos by Marc Crabtree except:
© ShutterStock.com/Tammy McAllister: page 14
Comstock: page 20 (meat, milk, and egg)
Corel: page 6
Ingram Photo Objects: page 20 (chocolate)

Illustrations
Margaret Amy Salter: page 20

Library and Archives Canada Cataloguing in Publication

MacAulay, Kelley
    Cocker spaniels / Kelley MacAulay & Bobbie Kalman.

(Pet care)
Includes index.
ISBN-13: 978-0-7787-1760-7 (bound)
ISBN-10: 0-7787-1760-7 (bound)
ISBN-13: 978-0-7787-1792-8 (pbk.)
ISBN1-: 0-7787-1792-5 (pbk.)
    1. Cocker spaniels--Juvenile literature. I. Kalman, Bobbie, date.
II. Title. III. Series: Pet care

SF429.C55M33 2006   j636.752'4   C2006-904093-1

Library of Congress Cataloging-in-Publication Data

MacAulay, Kelley.
    Cocker spaniels / Kelley MacAulay & Bobbie Kalman ; photographs by
Marc Crabtree.
        p. cm. -- (Pet care)
    Includes index.
    ISBN-13: 978-0-7787-1760-7 (rlb)
    ISBN-10: 0-7787-1760-7 (rlb)
    ISBN-13: 978-0-7787-1792-8 (pbk)
    ISBN-10: 0-7787-1792-5 (pbk)
    1. Cocker spaniels--Juvenile literature. I. Kalman, Bobbie. II. Title.
III. Series.

SF429.C55M23 2006
636.752'4--dc22

2006018062

Crabtree Publishing Company

www.crabtreebooks.com   1-800-387-7650

Copyright © **2007 CRABTREE PUBLISHING COMPANY.** All rights reserved. No part of this publication may be reproduced, stored in a retrieval system or be transmitted in any form or by any means, electronic, mechanical, photocopying, recording, or otherwise, without the prior written permission of Crabtree Publishing Company. In Canada: We acknowledge the financial support of the Government of Canada through the Book Publishing Industry Development Program (BPIDP) for our publishing activities.

Published in Canada
Crabtree Publishing
616 Welland Ave.
St. Catharines, ON
L2M 5V6

Published in the United States
Crabtree Publishing
PMB16A
350 Fifth Ave., Suite 3308
New York, NY 10118

Published in the United Kingdom
Crabtree Publishing
White Cross Mills
High Town, Lancaster
LA1 4XS

Published in Australia
Crabtree Publishing
386 Mt. Alexander Rd.
Ascot Vale (Melbourne)
VIC 3032

J
636.7524
M117

Contents

What are cocker spaniels?

Cocker spaniels are a **breed**, or type, of dog. Dogs are **mammals**. Mammals are animals that have **backbones**. A backbone is a row of bones in the middle of an animal's back. Mammals have hair or fur on their bodies. A baby mammal drinks milk from its mother's body.

A cocker spaniel's body

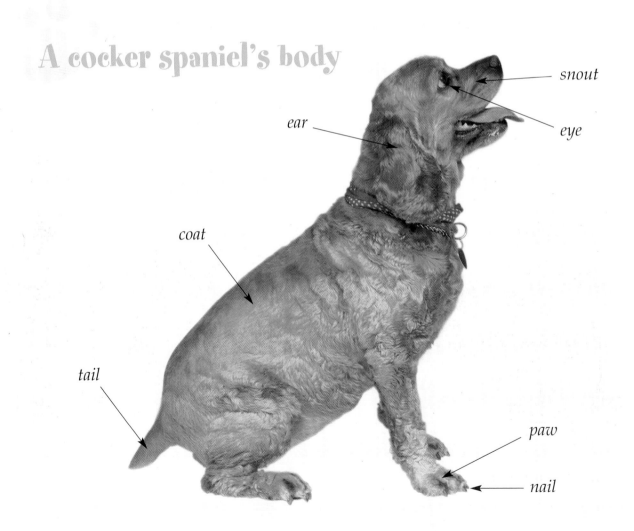

snout

ear

eye

coat

tail

paw

nail

4

Beautiful coats

Cocker spaniels are small dogs. Most cocker spaniels grow to be thirteen to sixteen inches (33-41 cm) tall. They weigh between 24 and 28 pounds (11-13 kg). Cocker spaniels are well-known for their beautiful, silky coats. The coats can be different colors, including black, **tan**, **buff**, and **chocolate**. Some cocker spaniels have coats that are two colors. Coats that are two colors are called **parti-colored coats**.

parti-colored
cocker spaniel

chocolate
cocker spaniel

buff cocker spaniel

black cocker spaniel

The history of cocker spaniels

Cocker spaniels are originally from England. For hundreds of years, English cocker spaniels helped hunters catch birds called woodcocks. "Cocker" spaniels are named after woodcocks. Today, English cocker spaniels are popular **show dogs**. Show dogs are dogs that people enter into competitions. The dogs are judged on how they look and on their ability to do tricks.

English cocker spaniel

Traveling to America

People brought English cocker spaniels to America in the early 1800s. Americans loved these dogs! People in America became **breeders** of cocker spaniels. By the 1900s, there were two breeds of cocker spaniels—English cocker spaniels and American cocker spaniels. This book is about American cocker spaniels. American cocker spaniels have shorter heads and thicker coats than English cocker spaniels have.

American cocker spaniel

The right pet for you?

Most cocker spaniels are friendly dogs. They love to play. Cocker spaniels require a lot of care and attention, however. Keeping their coats beautiful takes hard work! You will have to spend time every day **grooming**, or brushing and cleaning, your cocker spaniel. You will also have to feed and walk your pet every day. Would you take good care of a cocker spaniel?

Cocker spaniels usually live for twelve to fifteen years. Will you care for your pet for many years?

Are you ready?

Before you add a cocker spaniel to your family, gather everyone together and answer the questions below.

- Are you willing to groom your cocker spaniel every day to keep it healthy and looking neat?

- Cocker spaniels love attention! Will you make sure your cocker spaniel gets all the attention it needs?

- Who will feed your cocker spaniel every day?

- It costs a lot of money each year to feed a cocker spaniel and to take it to a **veterinarian** and a **dog groomer**. Is your family willing to pay for all your cocker spaniel's needs?

- **Training** a cocker spaniel can take a lot of time. Are you willing to work hard at training your pet?

- Cocker spaniels need exercise. Will you walk your dog every day?

Making friends

Cocker spaniels hate to be alone! If they are left alone for too long, they often misbehave. They may bark a lot or chew on your belongings.  Will someone be home with your cocker spaniel during the day? If not, you may want to get two cocker spaniels. They will keep each other company. Keep in mind that caring for two cocker spaniels will be twice the work, however!

Getting along

Do you have other pets? In time, your cocker spaniel may become friendly with your other pets. Some cocker spaniels even become friendly with cats! Cocker spaniels love to chase things, however. Be careful when introducing your cocker spaniel to your other pets. Do not force the animals together. If you are introducing a cocker spaniel to a cat, make sure the cat has a safe place to escape if the dog chases it.

Until your cocker spaniel is friendly with your other pets, never leave them alone together.

Choosing a cocker spaniel

If you are sure a cocker spaniel is the right pet for you, ask your friends and your veterinarian, or "vet," if they know of any cocker spaniels that are being given away. An **animal shelter** in your area may have a cocker spaniel. You can also get your cocker spaniel from a breeder or a pet store. Make sure you get your pet from someone who takes excellent care of animals!

Purebred pets

Some people prefer **purebred** dogs. A purebred dog has parents and grandparents of the same breed. If you want proof that your cocker spaniel is purebred, you should get your pet from a breeder. A good breeder can give you papers that prove your cocker spaniel's parents and grandparents were also cocker spaniels.

Pick a healthy pet

Choose a cocker spaniel that is healthy and friendly. The dog you choose should have:

- a damp nose

- clean teeth

- clear, shiny eyes

- clean ears with no wax inside

- a clean snout, coat, and bottom

- a shiny coat with no bald patches

- no sores on its skin

- a lot of energy

- a friendly, curious personality

A cocker spaniel may be shy at first. Do not rush toward the dog. Hold out your hand and let the dog come to you. Soon you will be good friends!

Caring for puppies

Do you want an adult cocker spaniel or do you want a **puppy**? A puppy is a baby dog. Cocker-spaniel puppies are cute and soft. It is easy to become attached to them!

Caring for puppies is more work than caring for dogs, however. Puppies chew on things and often **whine**, or cry, at night. They need several daily feedings. Someone must be with puppies at all times.

To be healthy, a cocker-spaniel puppy should stay with its mother for the first eight weeks of its life.

Housebreaking your pup

You will have to **housebreak** your cocker-spaniel puppy. Dogs that are housebroken know to go to the bathroom outdoors. To housebreak your puppy, put it on its leash and take it outdoors about ten minutes after it eats or drinks. Take your puppy to the same place each time. Praise your puppy when it goes to the bathroom outdoors. If you are **consistent** in the training, your puppy will learn to get your attention when it needs to go outdoors.

If you get an older cocker spaniel, it may be housebroken already. If your new pet is not housebroken, you must train it yourself.

What you will need

You will need certain supplies to care for your cocker spaniel properly. Make sure you have all the supplies before you bring home your new pet.

Your cocker spaniel will need a bowl for water and a bowl for food.

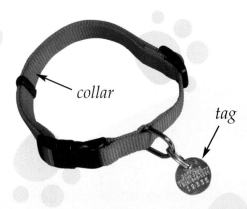

collar

tag

*Your pet should always wear a **collar** and a **tag** with your phone number on it. Your vet can also use a needle to place a small **microchip** that has your address in it under your dog's skin. If your pet gets lost, people can use the tag or microchip to return your pet to you.*

Attach a leash to the collar to keep your pet from running away.

Get a toothbrush and toothpaste made for dogs. Use them to keep your cocker spaniel's teeth healthy.

*You will need a **bristle brush** to groom your cocker spaniel's thick coat.*

*Get **nail clippers** made for dogs so an adult can trim your cocker spaniel's nails.*

Your cocker spaniel will need its own bed.

Buy some treats for your pet. You can use the treats as rewards when you train your cocker spaniel.

*A **crate** will give your cocker spaniel a **den**, or a safe place of its own.*

Your cocker spaniel should always have toys to play with and to chew on. Most cocker spaniels love chasing balls.

17

Home at last!

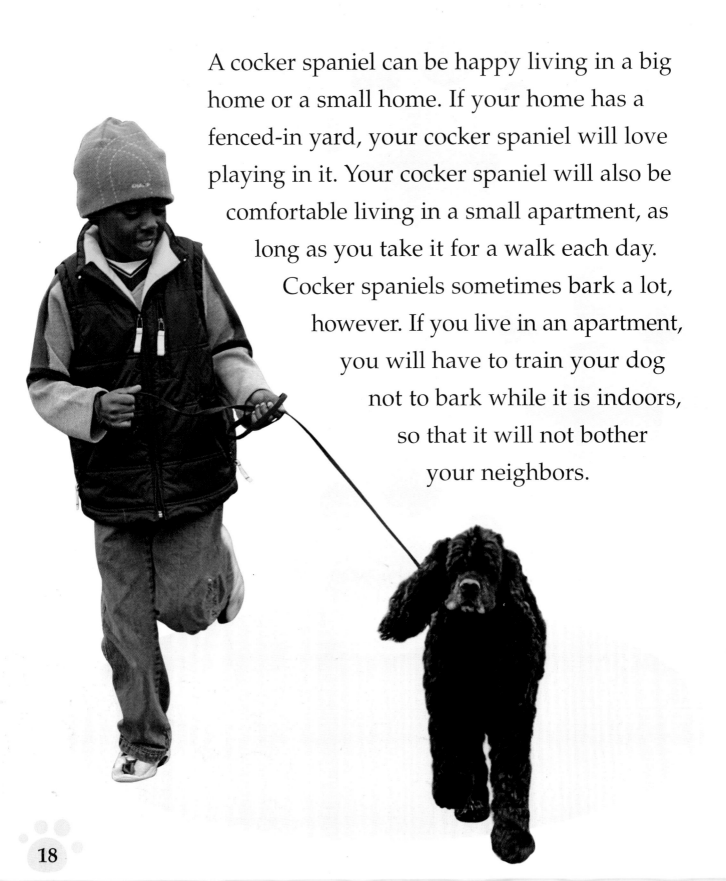

A cocker spaniel can be happy living in a big home or a small home. If your home has a fenced-in yard, your cocker spaniel will love playing in it. Your cocker spaniel will also be comfortable living in a small apartment, as long as you take it for a walk each day. Cocker spaniels sometimes bark a lot, however. If you live in an apartment, you will have to train your dog not to bark while it is indoors, so that it will not bother your neighbors.

Let me in!

If your house has a fenced-in yard, your cocker spaniel can spend some time outdoors by itself. Cocker spaniels do not like to be outdoors all the time, however. They need to be with people. Do not leave your cocker spaniel outdoors all the time.

Your pet will be unhappy if it is alone for long periods of time—indoors or outdoors! Find ways to spend time with your cocker spaniel.

Time for dinner!

Feed your cocker spaniel twice a day. Ask your vet how much food you should give your pet. Your vet can also tell you which brand of food is healthiest for your pet.

Feed your dog at the same time each morning and evening.

Unhealthy foods

Some foods can make your cocker spaniel sick. Do not feed your pet any of the foods listed below.

- Eating chocolate makes dogs very sick.

- **Dairy foods** are not healthy for dogs.

- Do not give your cocker spaniel bones to chew on. It could choke on them.

- Never feed your dog **raw** meat or raw eggs!

Fresh water

Make sure your cocker spaniel always has a full bowl of fresh water to drink. Your pet does not need to drink anything other than water. Wash your pet's food and water dishes every day.

Feeding a puppy

To feed a puppy, soak dry puppy food in hot water to make it soft. Let the food cool before giving it to the puppy. Cocker-spaniel puppies need to be fed four times a day until they are three months old. Puppies that are between three and six months old need to eat three times a day. When your cocker spaniel is six months old, it can begin eating twice a day.

Pretty pooches

Cocker spaniels make great pets, but they require more grooming than some other dog breeds do. Their long, curly coats tangle easily. You will have to groom your cocker spaniel every day. These pages will help you keep your cocker spaniel looking spiffy! An adult should help you with some of these jobs.

*Gently brush your pet every day with a bristle brush. Take your pet to a groomer to have its fur **clipped**, or cut, every four to six weeks.*

Bath time!

Give your cocker spaniel a bath every six to eight weeks. Gently rub a small amount of dog shampoo into your pet's coat. Make sure you rinse out all the shampoo. Next, rub a dog conditioner into your pet's coat. Wash out the conditioner thoroughly. Using conditioner will make it easier to brush your cocker spaniel after its bath.

Neat nails

If your pet's nails are clicking on the floor, ask an adult to cut them. Only the very end of each nail should be cut. If too much is cut off, the nail will bleed. If bleeding occurs, use **styptic powder** to stop the bleeding. If the nail continues to bleed after using the powder, take your pet to the vet right away.

Gently pull up the sides of your cocker spaniel's mouth each day. Make sure there are no sores and no dried food on the sides of its mouth. Then brush your cocker spaniel's teeth with a toothbrush and toothpaste made for dogs.

Cocker spaniels often develop problems in their ears. Every day, gently lift each ear and look inside. If your pet scratches its ears a lot, or if there is a lot of wax in the ears, take your pet to the vet.

Training your pet

You will have to spend at least fifteen minutes each day training your cocker spaniel. It can be difficult to train cocker spaniels, however! They are distracted easily. You may have to teach your cocker spaniel the same **commands**, or instructions, many times before it remembers them.

If your cocker spaniel does not sit down, press gently on its bottom while saying "sit."

Begin with the basics

You should train your cocker spaniel to "sit." To teach your dog to sit, show it a treat. Then move the hand that is holding the treat back over your cocker spaniel's head. Say "sit" as you move your hand. Your cocker spaniel will sit down in order to look up and see its treat. Once your pet is sitting, give it the treat and a lot of praise!

Gentle training

Cocker spaniels are sensitive dogs. They become nervous easily. Never hit or yell at your cocker spaniel, or it will become afraid of you. Use gentle words and a lot of praise when talking to your pet. After training, make time to play with your cocker spaniel.

School days

If you find it difficult to train your cocker spaniel, you can take it to an **obedience school**, or a school for training dogs. The trainers at obedience school can teach you how to get your pet to behave. You and your pet will learn many commands.

You can teach your cocker spaniel to do tricks! This cocker spaniel has learned to "turn around".

Fun and games

Your cocker spaniel needs to have toys so that it can play by itself. Cocker spaniels get bored easily. If you do not give your pet toys, it will use some of your belongings as toys! Give your dog about five toys. Keep other toys tucked away. To keep your pet interested, change its toys about once a month. If the dog has a favorite toy, do not take that one away.

Certain toys are safer for your pet than others. Chew toys made of rubber are a good choice. Do not give your cocker spaniel small balls that it could choke on.

Where is my owner?

Cocker spaniels are active dogs. They like to play games with people. A fun game to play with your cocker spaniel is hide-and-seek. To play hide-and-seek, have a friend hold your cocker spaniel gently while you hide. Once you are hidden, call out to your pet. It will have fun trying to find you. Praise your cocker spaniel when it finds you.

Only play hide-and-seek with your cocker spaniel inside your home or in a fenced-in yard. If you are in an open area outdoors, you will not be able to watch your pet carefully as it runs around looking for you.

Safety first

Cocker spaniels love to be with people, but they still need their own space. There are times when you should not bother your pet, such as while it is eating. Your cocker spaniel may become **aggressive**, or angry, if you try to take away its food or its favorite toy. An aggressive dog may bite to protect its space.

Your cocker spaniel may go inside its crate when it needs to rest. You should leave your pet alone when it is in its crate.

Watch out!

If your cocker spaniel becomes aggressive, it may attack you or another person. If your dog is about to attack, it may growl, show its teeth, and stare at you. If your dog behaves this way, do not run away. Look at the ground and hold your arms at your sides. Say "good dog" in a soothing voice to try to calm down the dog. When the dog calms down, tell an adult how the dog behaved.

When introducing your friends to your pet, ask them to remain calm and to speak quietly until your pet gets used to them.

Veterinary care

As soon as you get a cocker spaniel, take it to a vet. The vet will check the dog to make sure it is healthy. When necessary, the vet will give your pet **vaccinations** with needles. The vaccinations will protect your cocker spaniel from becoming ill. Take your cocker spaniel to the vet for a checkup every year.

No unwanted puppies!

You should have your cocker spaniel **neutered**. A neutered dog cannot make puppies. If you let your cocker spaniel have puppies, you will have to work hard to care for the puppies and find them good homes.

As cocker spaniels get older, they often develop health problems. Ask your vet about warning signs that show your dog is becoming ill.

Be aware

If your cocker spaniel seems sick, take it to a vet right away. Watch for the warning signs listed below.

- Your cocker spaniel should go to the vet if it is vomiting, fainting, or limping.

- Your cocker spaniel may be sick if it is losing clumps of fur.

- Your cocker spaniel's ears and eyes should be clean, and you should not feel any lumps on its body.

- A sick cocker spaniel may drink more water than usual. It may also stop eating.

- If your cocker spaniel is sleeping more than usual and is not playful, take it to the vet.

Your cocker spaniel will be happy to be your best friend! By providing it with the proper care, your dog will live a long, happy life with you.

Words to know

Note: Boldfaced words that are defined in the book may not appear on this page.

animal shelter A place that cares for animals that do not have owners

breeder A person who brings dogs together so that the dogs can make puppies

buff A yellowish-beige color

chocolate A dark brown color

consistent Describing behavior that does not change over time

dairy food Food made with milk and milk products

dog groomer A person who cleans and brushes dogs for a living

microchip A small device that can hold information, which can be placed under an animal's skin

raw Describing foods that are not cooked

styptic powder A powder that stops a dog's nails from bleeding

tan A yellowish-brown color

train To teach a dog how to behave properly

vaccination A way of protecting a body against diseases

veterinarian A doctor who treats animals

Index

1 2 3 4 5 6 7 8 9 0   Printed in the U.S.A.   5 4 3 2 1 0 9 8 7 6